Design & Layout by Brittany Mays of bmays.com

konnectwithdrkim.com

Self-Care
Journal

Self-Care is an intentional act. It involves taking time for yourself daily and having a routine. I would like for this journal to be self-inspired with some guidance on what I have found self-care to be. There are six domains of self-care that I would like for you to be mindful of as you begin your wonderful, exciting, and diligent journey called self-care. My vision is to nurture you in becoming whole (Body, Soul, Spirit, and Mind) through the use of self-care.

Enjoy!

Kim Alderson, DSW, LCSW

Reflection

Here is where you begin by finding out where you are and growing from there. These domains are for guidance. Implement at your own pace.

Physical Self-Care

Examples:
- Eating on a regular basis
- Getting routine medical
- Check-ups
- Exercise
- Get enough sleep
- Take a break

Emotional Self-Care

Examples:
- Write in a journal
- Have quiet time
- Connect with a therapist
- Self-reflection
- Say no
- Love yourself
- Laugh
- Cry

Social Self-Care

Examples:
- Hang out with others
- Check on family and friends
- Listen to music
- Watch a movie
- Read a book
- Go to a play or museum

Professional Self-Care

Examples:
- Take a break during the day
- Don't eat lunch at your desk
- Say no
- Have boundaries
- Negotiate your needs
- Make your office space comfortable
- Talk to your co-workers

Spiritual Self-Care

Examples:
- Meditate
- Pray
- Enjoy experiences of awe
- Be open to inspiration
- Talk to you spiritual leader

Financial Self-Care

Examples:
- Plan
- Budget
- Spend more
- Spend less

SELF-CURE

Putting the "U" in Self-Care

A
Healthier
YOU

SOCIAL

SPIRITUAL

FINANCIAL

PROFESSIONAL

EMOTIONAL

PHYSICAL

Week of:

Sunday

Monday

Tuesday

Wednesday

Thursday

Friday

Saturday

Notes:

Notes:

Notes:

Notes:

Notes:

Notes:

Notes:

My Aspirations
THIS WEEK

Journal

Journal

Week of:

Sunday

Monday

Tuesday

Wednesday

Thursday

Friday

Saturday

Notes:

Notes:

Notes:

Notes:

Notes:

Notes:

Notes:

My Aspirations
THIS WEEK

Journal

Journal

Free Art Space

Week of:

Sunday

Monday

Tuesday

Wednesday

Thursday

Friday

Saturday

Notes:

Notes:

Notes:

Notes:

Notes:

Notes:

Notes:

My Aspirations
THIS WEEK

Journal

Journal

ENJOY
THE
JOURNEY

Sunday

Monday

Tuesday

Wednesday

Thursday

Friday

Saturday

Notes:

Notes:

Notes:

Notes:

Notes:

Notes:

Notes:

My Aspirations
THIS WEEK

Journal

Journal

Journal

Free Art Space

My Accomplishments
THIS MONTH

_____
_____
_____
_____
_____
_____
_____
_____

Areas of Growth
FOR NEXT MONTH

_____
_____
_____
_____
_____
_____
_____
_____

Sunday

Monday

Tuesday

Wednesday

Thursday

Friday

Saturday

Notes:

Notes:

Notes:

Notes:

Notes:

Notes:

Notes:

My Aspirations
THIS WEEK

Journal

Journal

SELF-CARE IS KEY

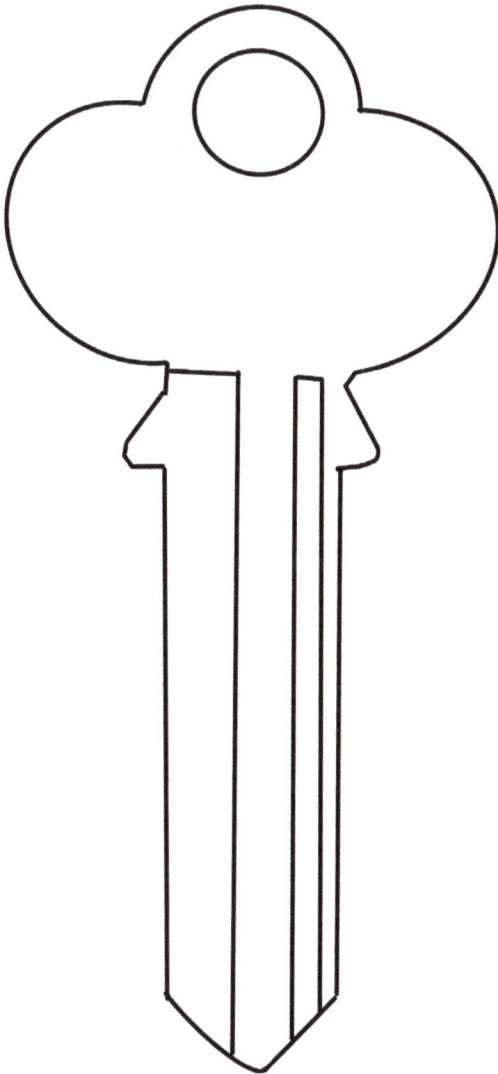

Week of:

Sunday

Monday

Tuesday

Wednesday

Thursday

Friday

Saturday

Notes:

Notes:

Notes:

Notes:

Notes:

Notes:

Notes:

My Aspirations
THIS WEEK

Journal

Journal

Free Art Space

Week of:

Sunday

Monday

Tuesday

Wednesday

Thursday

Friday

Saturday

Notes:

Notes:

Notes:

Notes:

Notes:

Notes:

Notes:

My Aspirations
THIS WEEK

Journal

_____
_____
_____
_____
_____
_____
_____
_____
_____
_____
_____
_____
_____
_____
_____
_____
_____
_____
_____
_____
_____
_____
_____
_____
_____
_____
_____

Journal

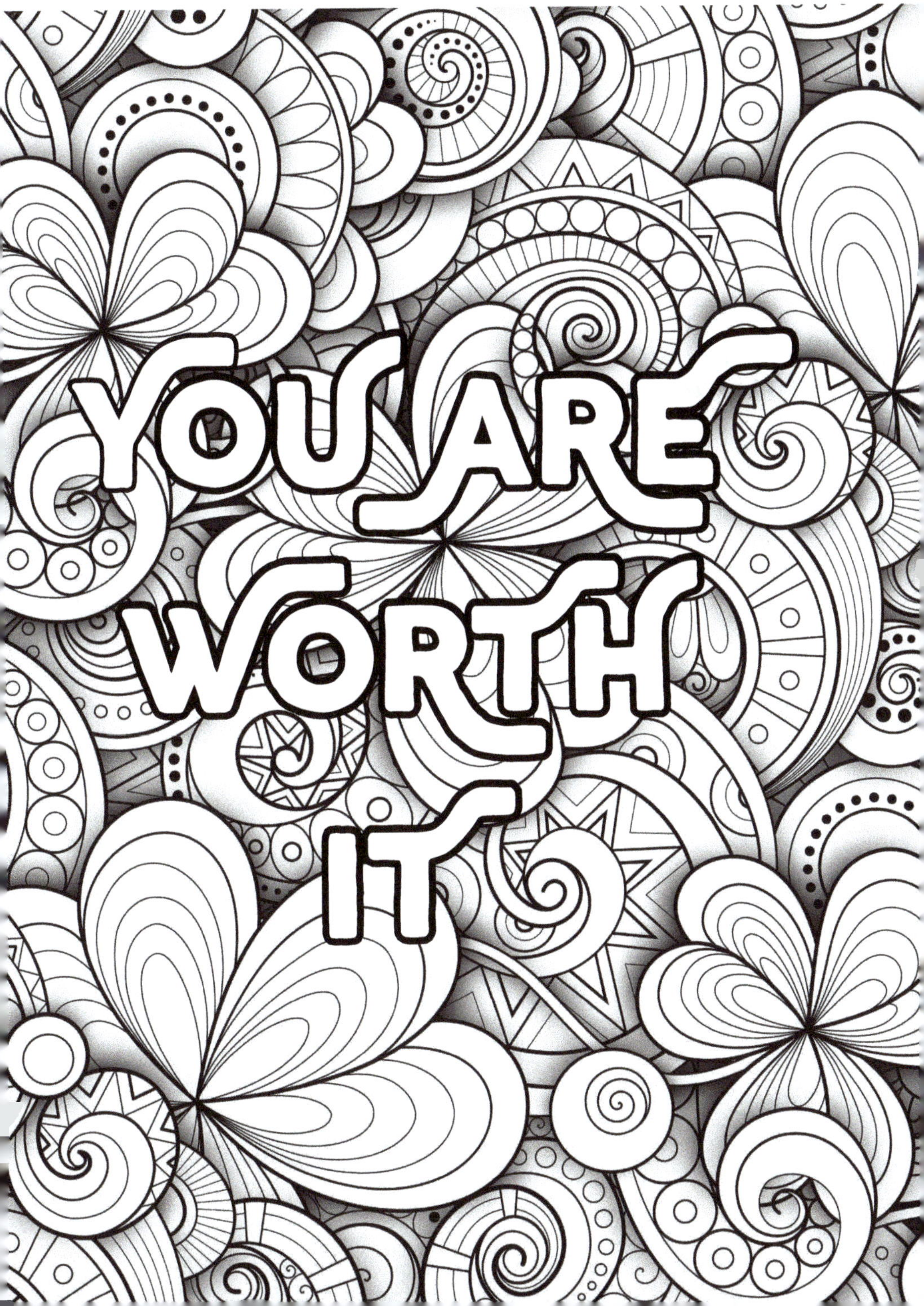
YOU ARE
WORTH
IT

Week of:

Sunday

Monday

Tuesday

Wednesday

Thursday

Friday

Saturday

Notes:

Notes:

Notes:

Notes:

Notes:

Notes:

Notes:

My Aspirations
THIS WEEK

Journal

Journal

Journal

Free Art Space

My Accomplishments
THIS MONTH

_____
_____
_____
_____
_____
_____
_____
_____

Areas of Growth
FOR NEXT MONTH

_____
_____
_____
_____
_____
_____
_____
_____

Week of:

Sunday

Monday

Tuesday

Wednesday

Thursday

Friday

Saturday

Take a Hot Shower/Bubble Bath

Notes:

Notes:

Notes:

Notes:

Notes:

Notes:

Notes:

My Aspirations
THIS WEEK

Journal

Journal

Week of:

Sunday

Monday

Tuesday

Wednesday

Thursday

Friday

Saturday

Notes:

Notes:

Notes:

Notes:

Notes:

Notes:

Notes:

My Aspirations
THIS WEEK

Journal

Journal

Free Art Space

Week of:

Sunday

Monday

Tuesday

Wednesday

Thursday

Friday

Saturday

Notes:

Notes:

Notes:

Notes:

Notes:

Notes:

Notes:

My Aspirations
THIS WEEK

Journal

Journal

YOU GOT THIS!

Sunday

Monday

Tuesday

Wednesday

Thursday

Friday

Saturday

Notes:

Notes:

Notes:

Notes:

Notes:

Notes:

Notes:

My Aspirations
THIS WEEK

Journal

Journal

Journal

Free Art Space

My Accomplishments
THIS MONTH

_____
_____
_____
_____
_____
_____
_____
_____

Areas of Growth
FOR NEXT MONTH

_____
_____
_____
_____
_____
_____
_____
_____

Sunday

Monday

Tuesday

Wednesday

Thursday

Friday

Saturday

Be Mindful

Notes:

Notes:

Notes:

Notes:

Notes:

Notes:

Notes:

My Aspirations
THIS WEEK

Journal

Journal

Week of:

Sunday

Monday

Tuesday

Wednesday

Thursday

Friday

Saturday

Notes:

Notes:

Notes:

Notes:

Notes:

Notes:

Notes:

My Aspirations
THIS WEEK

Journal

Journal

Free Art Space

Sunday

Monday

Tuesday

Wednesday

Thursday

Friday

Saturday

Notes:

Notes:

Notes:

Notes:

Notes:

Notes:

Notes:

My Aspirations
THIS WEEK

Journal

Journal

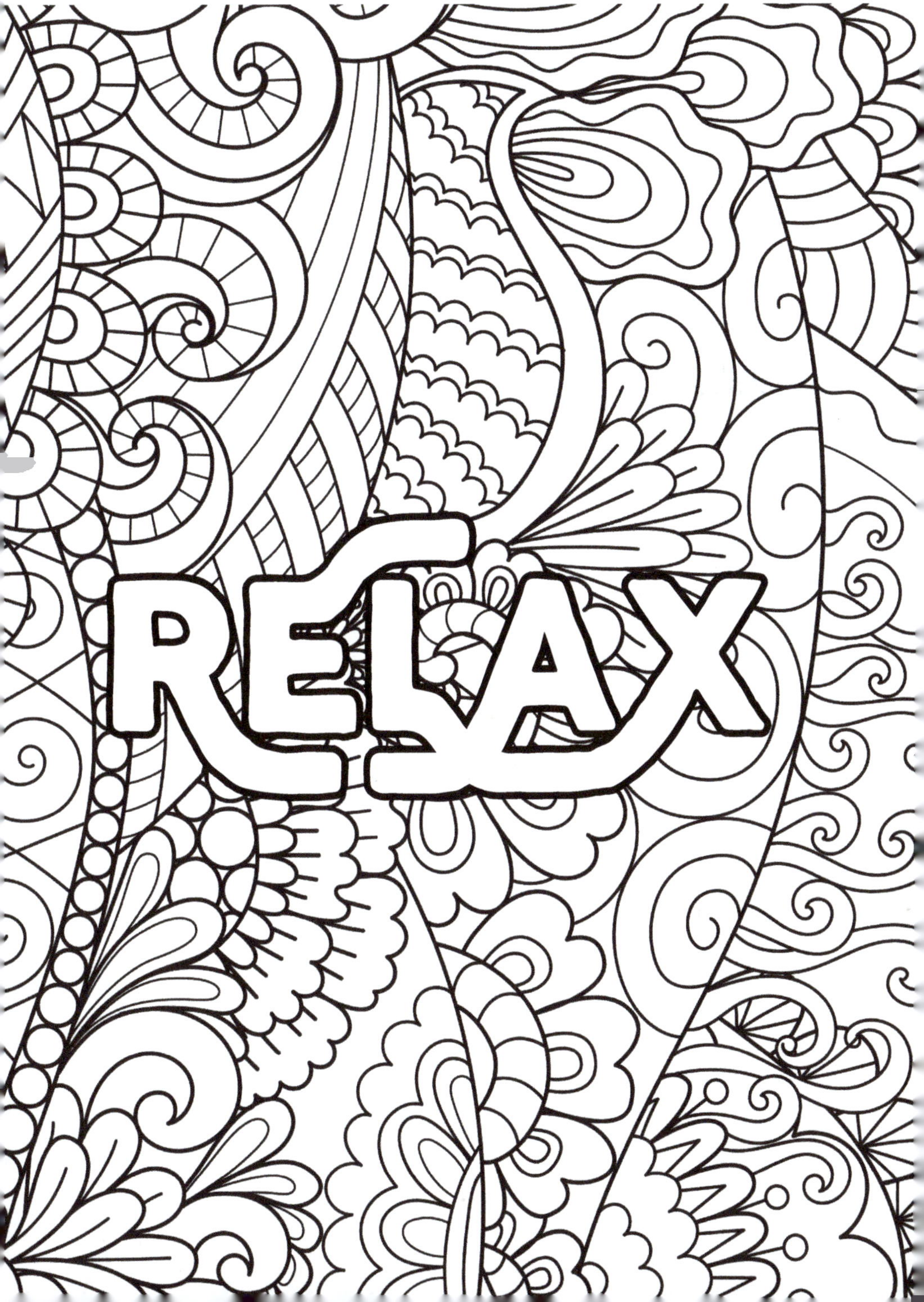
RELAX

Week of:

Sunday

Monday

Tuesday

Wednesday

Thursday

Friday

Saturday

Cry

Notes:

Notes:

Notes:

Notes:

Notes:

Notes:

Notes:

My Aspirations
THIS WEEK

Journal

Journal

Free Art Space

My Accomplishments
THIS MONTH

_____

_____

_____

_____

_____

_____

_____

_____

Areas of Growth
FOR NEXT MONTH

_____

_____

_____

_____

_____

_____

_____

_____

Sunday

Monday

Tuesday

Wednesday

Thursday

Friday

Saturday

Focus on Mental Health. Try Therapy

Notes:

Notes:

Notes:

Notes:

Notes:

Notes:

Notes:

My Aspirations
THIS WEEK

Journal

Journal

Week of:

Sunday

Monday

Tuesday

Wednesday

Thursday

Friday

Saturday

Notes:

Notes:

Notes:

Notes:

Notes:

Notes:

Notes:

My Aspirations
THIS WEEK

Journal

Journal

Free Art Space

Sunday

Monday

Tuesday

Wednesday

Thursday

Friday

Saturday

Notes:

Notes:

Notes:

Notes:

Notes:

Notes:

Notes:

My Aspirations
THIS WEEK

Journal

Journal

DON'T FEEL GUILTY ABOUT SELF-CARE

Sunday

Monday

Tuesday

Wednesday

Thursday

Friday

Saturday

Notes:

Notes:

Notes:

Notes:

Notes:

Notes:

Notes:

My Aspirations
THIS WEEK

Journal

Journal

Journal

Free Art Space

My Accomplishments
THIS MONTH

_____

_____

_____

_____

_____

_____

_____

_____

Areas of Growth
FOR NEXT MONTH

_____

_____

_____

_____

_____

_____

_____

_____

Week of:

Sunday

Monday

Tuesday

Wednesday

Thursday

Friday

Saturday

Notes:

Notes:

Notes:

Notes:

Notes:

Notes:

Notes:

My Aspirations
THIS WEEK

Journal

Journal

Week of:

Sunday

Monday

Tuesday

Wednesday

Thursday

Friday

Saturday

Notes:

Notes:

Notes:

Notes:

Notes:

Notes:

Notes:

My Aspirations
THIS WEEK

Journal

Journal

Free Art Space

Sunday

Monday

Tuesday

Wednesday

Thursday

Friday

Saturday

Notes:

Notes:

Notes:

Notes:

Notes:

Notes:

Notes:

My Aspirations
THIS WEEK

Journal

Journal

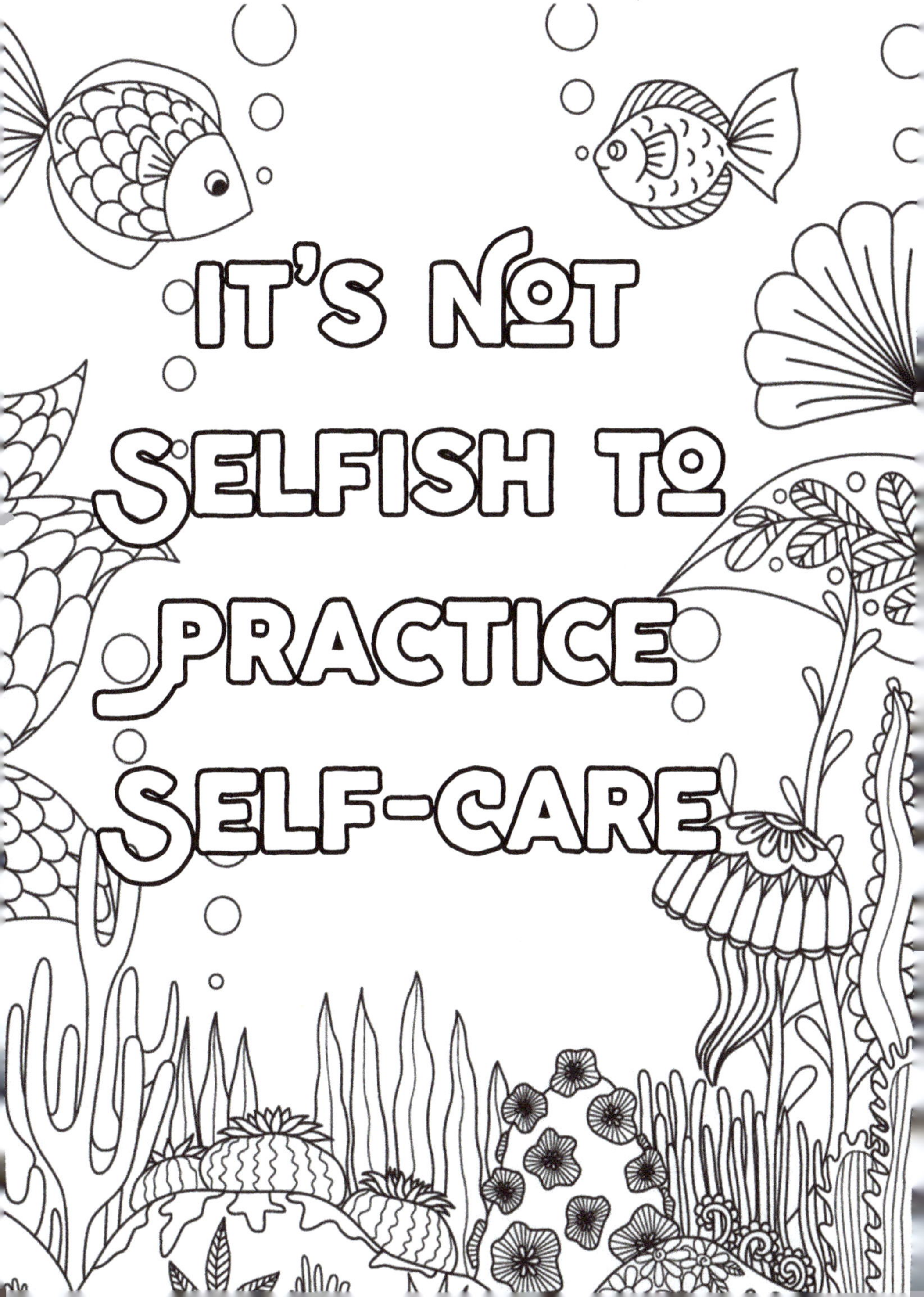
IT'S NOT
SELFISH TO
PRACTICE
SELF-CARE

Week of:

Sunday

Monday

Tuesday

Wednesday

Thursday

Friday

Saturday

Notes:

Notes:

Notes:

Notes:

Notes:

Notes:

Notes:

My Aspirations
THIS WEEK

Journal

Journal

Journal

Free Art Space

My Accomplishments
THIS MONTH

_____

_____

_____

_____

_____

_____

_____

Areas of Growth
FOR NEXT MONTH

_____

_____

_____

_____

_____

_____

_____

_____

Week of:

Sunday

Monday

Tuesday

Wednesday

Thursday

Friday

Saturday

Notes:

Notes:

Notes:

Notes:

Notes:

Notes:

Notes:

My Aspirations
THIS WEEK

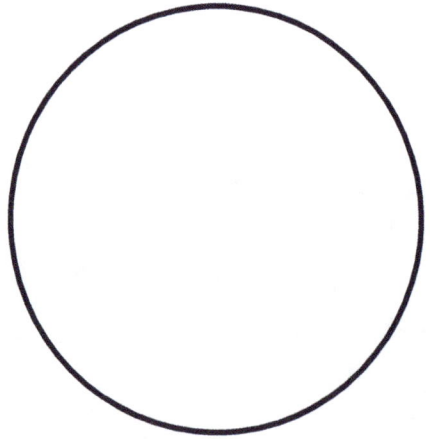

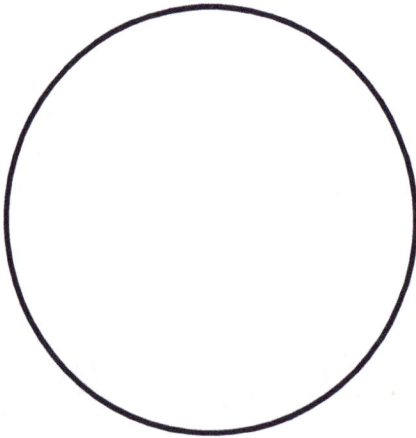

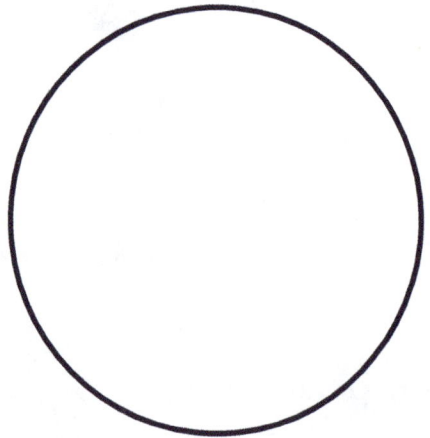

Journal

Journal

take care of yourself

Week of:

Sunday

Monday

Tuesday

Wednesday

Thursday

Friday

Saturday

Notes:

Notes:

Notes:

Notes:

Notes:

Notes:

Notes:

My Aspirations
THIS WEEK

Journal

Journal

Free Art Space

Sunday

Monday

Tuesday

Wednesday

Thursday

Friday

Saturday

Notes:

Notes:

Notes:

Notes:

Notes:

Notes:

Notes:

My Aspirations
THIS WEEK

Journal

Journal

KNOW YOUR WORTH

Sunday

Monday

Tuesday

Wednesday

Thursday

Friday

Saturday

Notes:

Notes:

Notes:

Notes:

Notes:

Notes:

Notes:

My Aspirations
THIS WEEK

Journal

Journal

Free Art Space

My Accomplishments
THIS MONTH

_____

_____

_____

_____

_____

_____

_____

_____

Areas of Growth
FOR NEXT MONTH

_____

_____

_____

_____

_____

_____

_____

_____

Week of:

Sunday

Monday

Tuesday

Wednesday

Thursday

Friday

Saturday

Notes:

Notes:

Notes:

Notes:

Notes:

Notes:

Notes:

My Aspirations
THIS WEEK

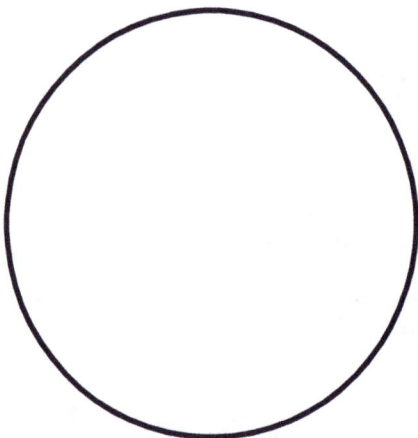

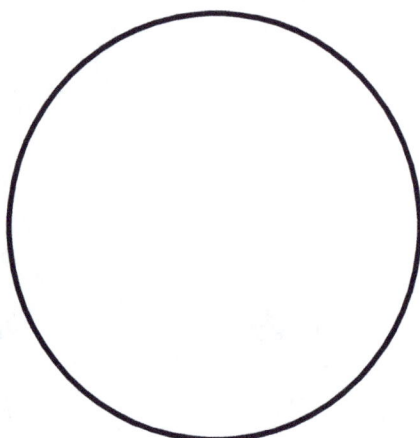

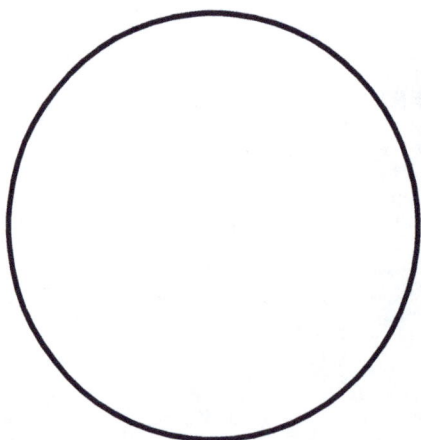

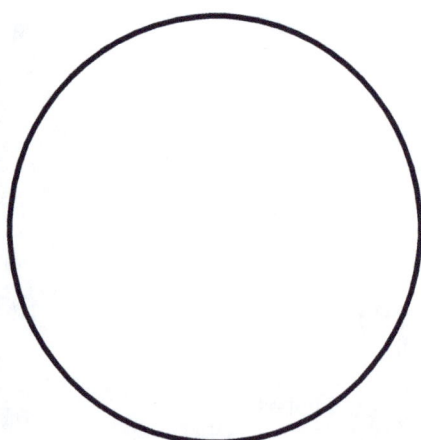

Journal

Journal

Week of:

Sunday

Monday

Tuesday

Wednesday

Thursday

Friday

Saturday

Notes:

Notes:

Notes:

Notes:

Notes:

Notes:

Notes:

My Aspirations
THIS WEEK

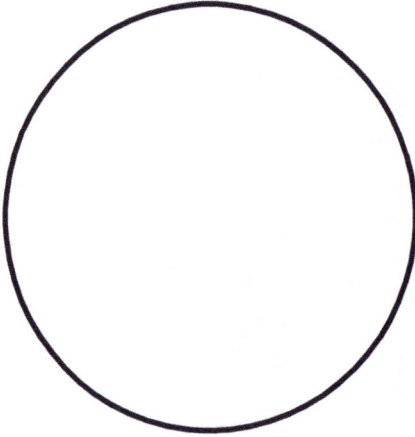

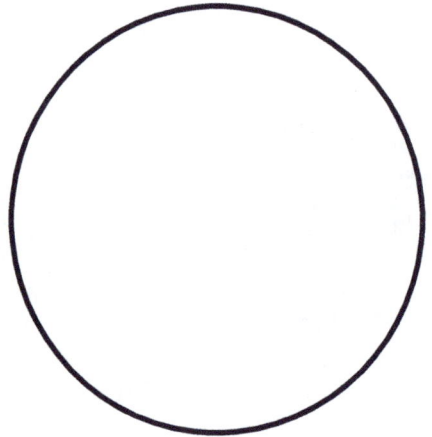

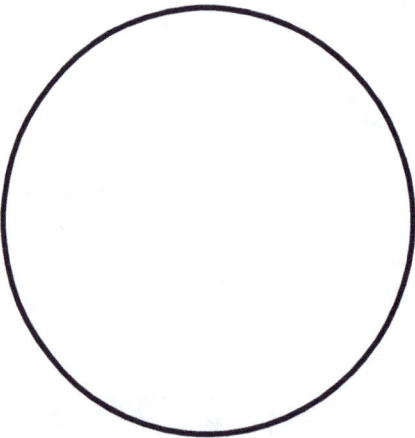

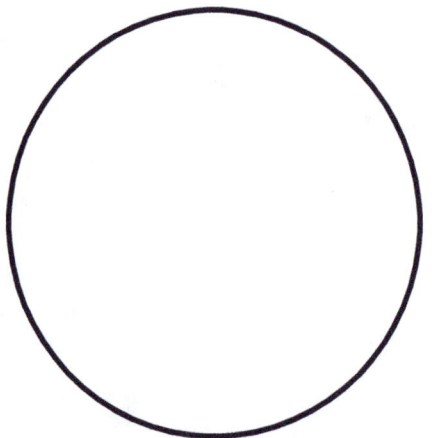

Journal

Free Art Space

Sunday

Monday

Tuesday

Wednesday

Thursday

Friday

Saturday

Notes:

Notes:

Notes:

Notes:

Notes:

Notes:

Notes:

My Aspirations
THIS WEEK

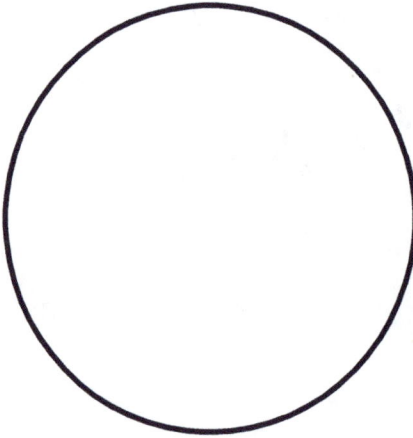

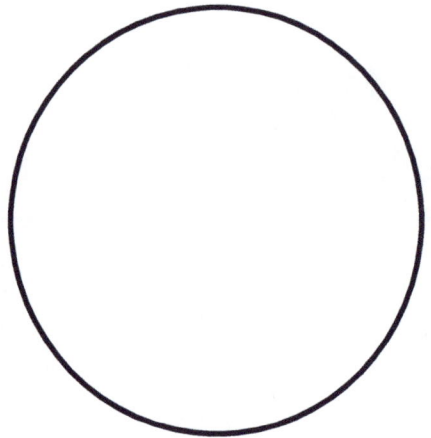

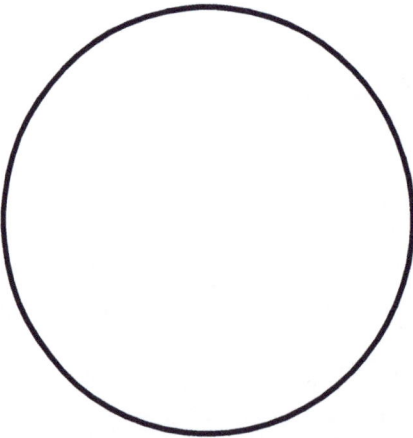

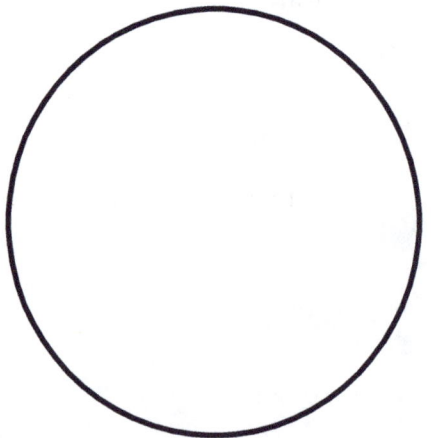

Journal

Journal

Week of:

Sunday

Monday

Tuesday

Wednesday

Thursday

Friday

Saturday

Notes:

Notes:

Notes:

Notes:

Notes:

Notes:

Notes:

My Aspirations
THIS WEEK

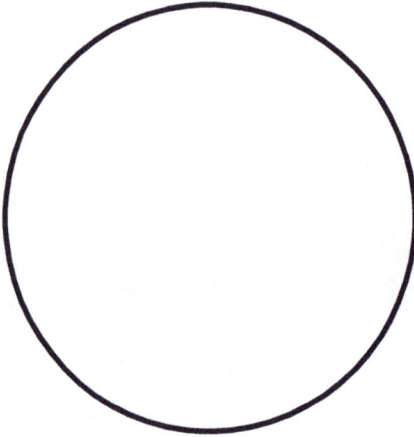

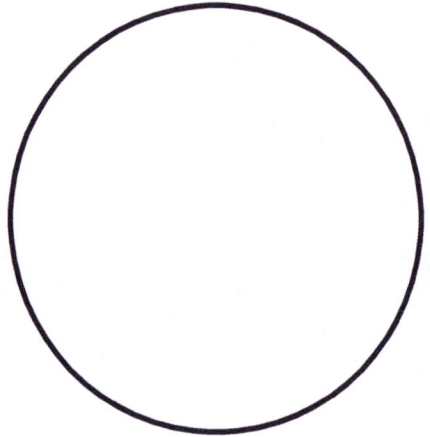

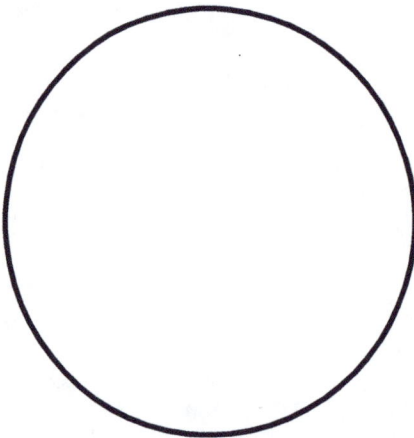

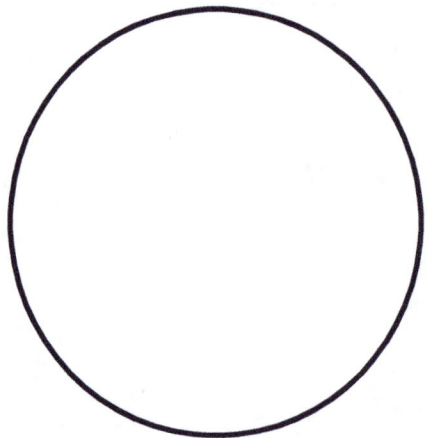

Journal

Journal

Journal

Art Therapy

Free Art Space

My Accomplishments
THIS MONTH

_____

_____

_____

_____

_____

_____

_____

_____

Areas of Growth
FOR NEXT MONTH

_____

_____

_____

_____

_____

_____

_____

_____

Week of:

Sunday

Monday

Tuesday

Wednesday

Thursday

Friday

Saturday

Priortz

Notes:

Notes:

Notes:

Notes:

Notes:

Notes:

Notes:

My Aspirations
THIS WEEK

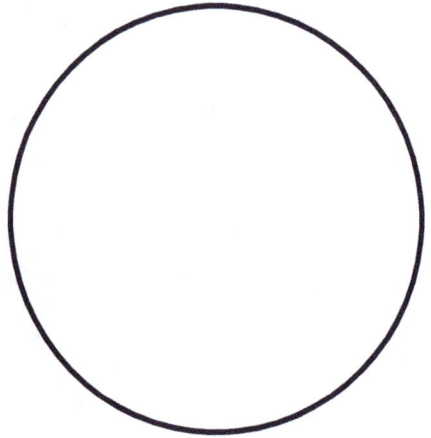

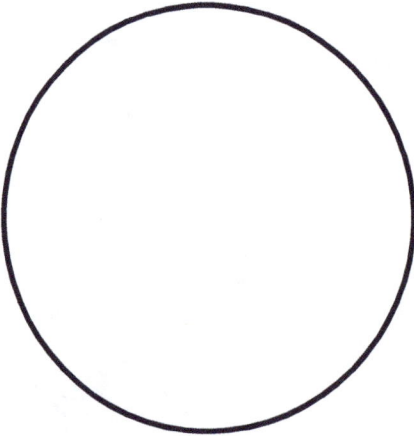

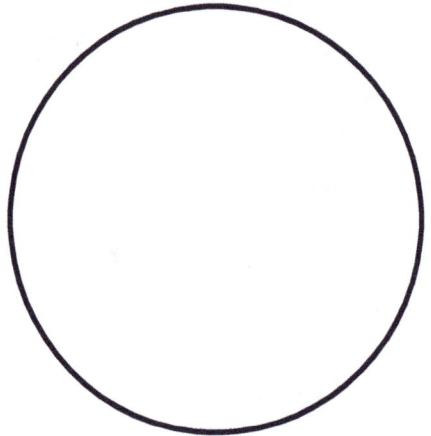

Journal

Journal

Week of:

Sunday

Monday

Tuesday

Wednesday

Thursday

Friday

Saturday

Notes:

Notes:

Notes:

Notes:

Notes:

Notes:

Notes:

My Aspirations
THIS WEEK

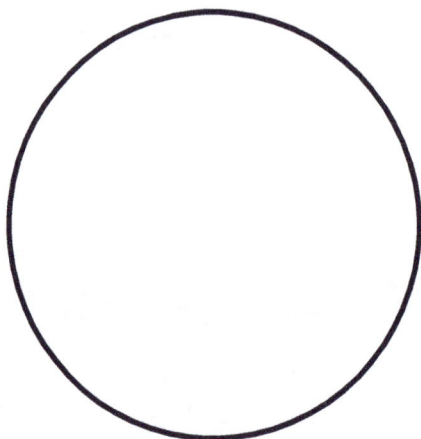

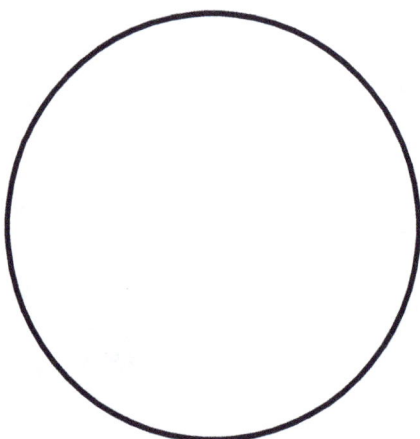

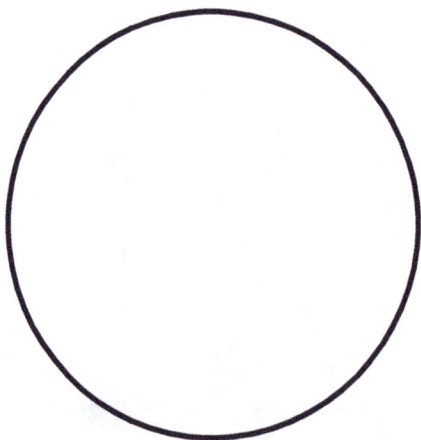

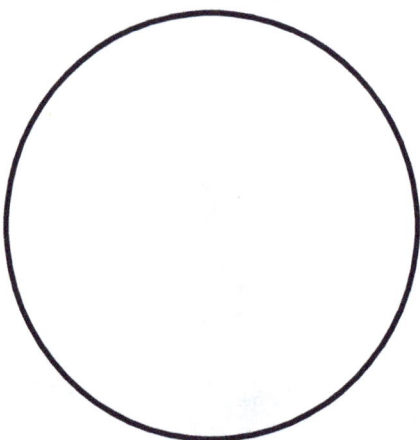

Journal

Journal

Free Art Space

Sunday

Monday

Tuesday

Wednesday

Thursday

Friday

Saturday

Notes:

Notes:

Notes:

Notes:

Notes:

Notes:

Notes:

My Aspirations
THIS WEEK

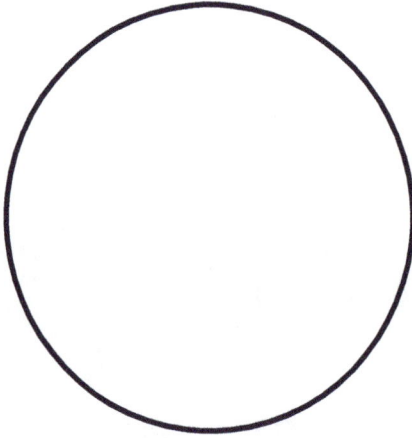

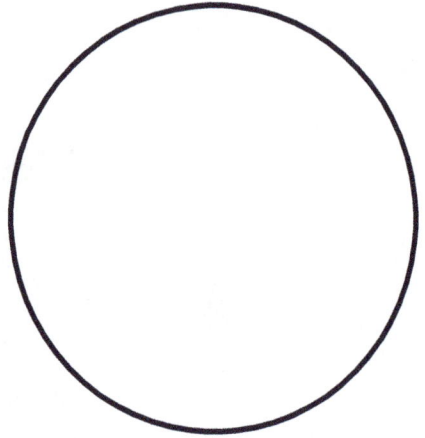

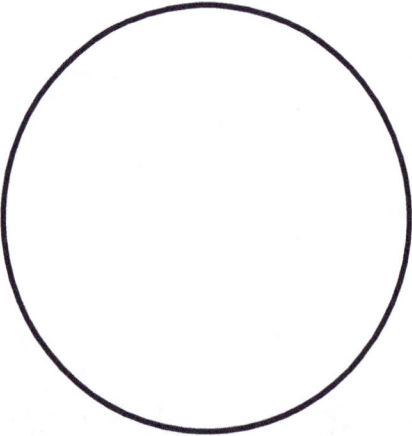

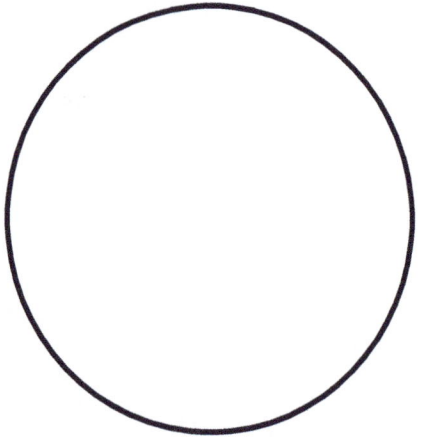

Journal

Journal

IT'S ALL
ABOUT
ME

Week of:

Sunday

Monday

Tuesday

Wednesday

Thursday

Friday

Saturday

Notes:

Notes:

Notes:

Notes:

Notes:

Notes:

Notes:

My Aspirations
THIS WEEK

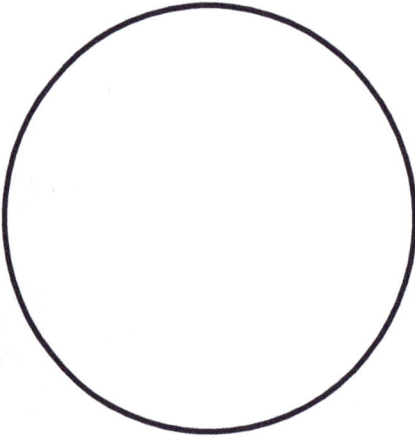

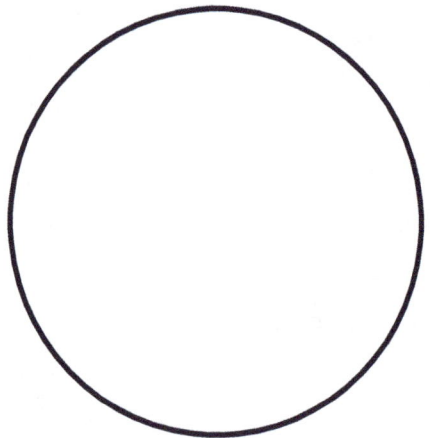

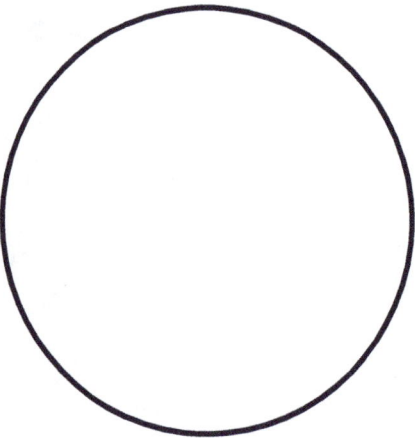

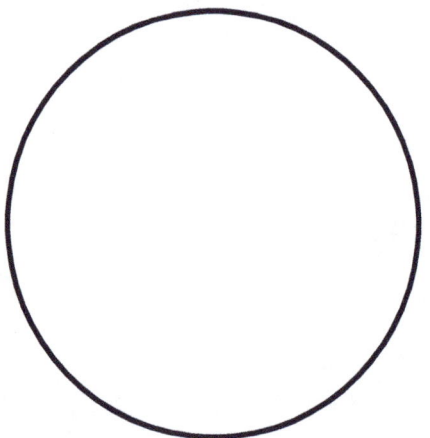

Journal

Journal

Journal

Free Art Space

My Accomplishments
THIS MONTH

_____

_____

_____

_____

_____

_____

_____

Areas of Growth
FOR NEXT MONTH

_____

_____

_____

_____

_____

_____

_____

_____

Sunday

Monday

Tuesday

Wednesday

Thursday

Friday

Saturday

Give Yourself Affirmations

Notes:

Notes:

Notes:

Notes:

Notes:

Notes:

Notes:

My Aspirations
THIS WEEK

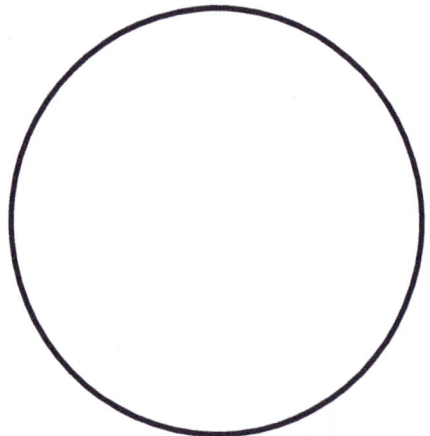

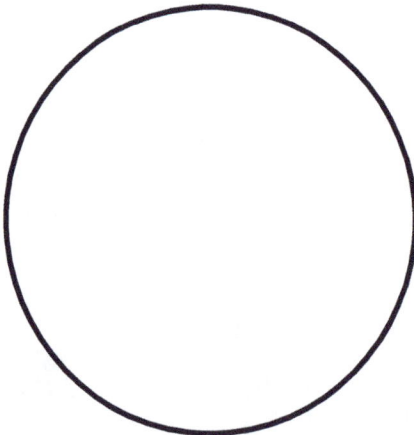

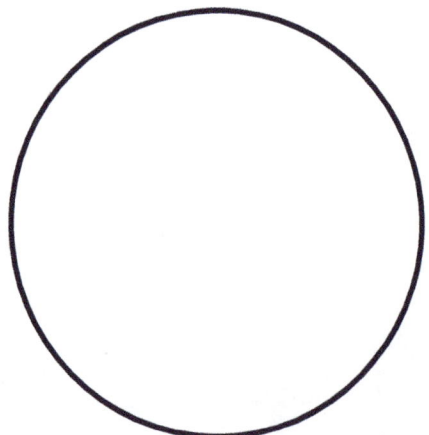

Journal

Journal

Sunday

Monday

Tuesday

Wednesday

Thursday

Friday

Saturday

Check In With Your Medical Professional

Notes:

Notes:

Notes:

Notes:

Notes:

Notes:

Notes:

My Aspirations
THIS WEEK

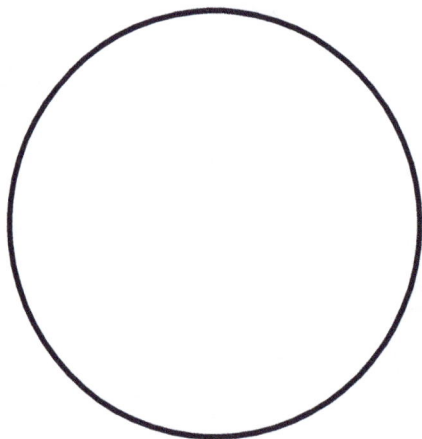

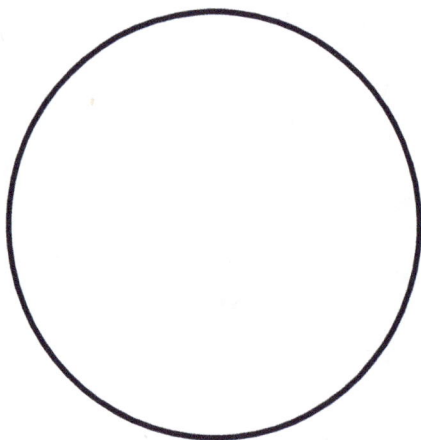

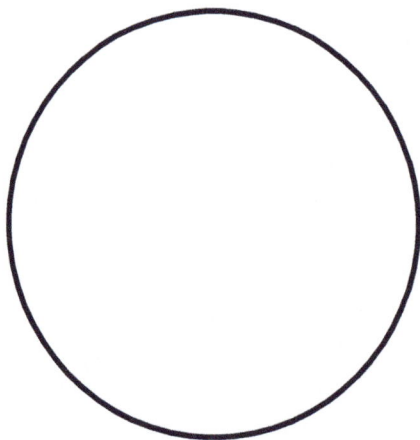

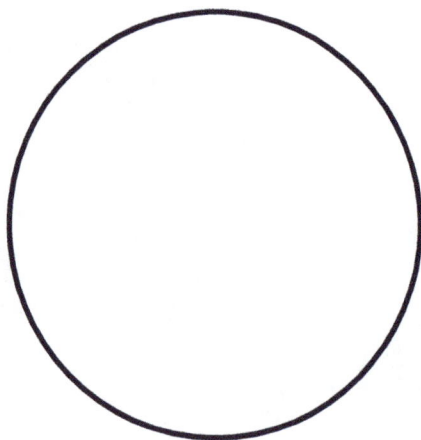

Journal

Journal

Free Art Space

Week of:

Sunday

Monday

Tuesday

Wednesday

Thursday

Friday

Saturday

Notes:

Notes:

Notes:

Notes:

Notes:

Notes:

Notes:

My Aspirations
THIS WEEK

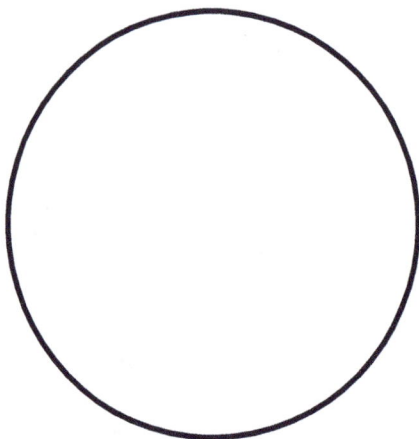

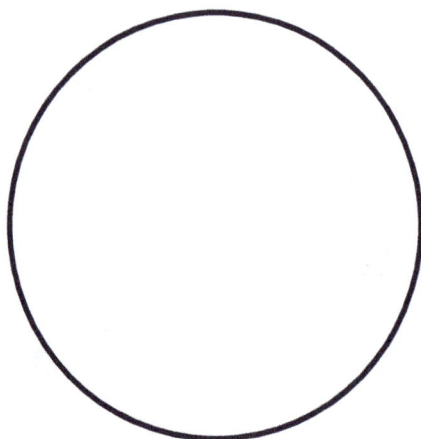

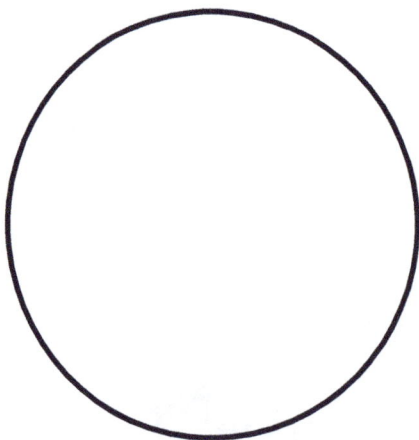

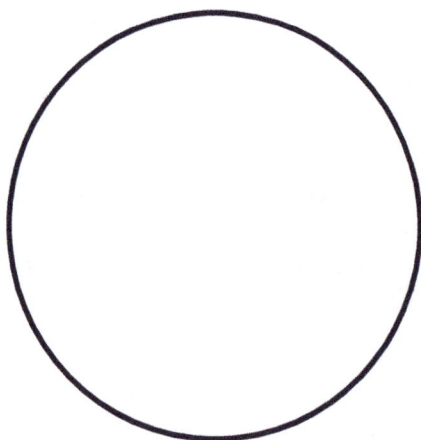

Journal

Journal

Sunday

Monday

Tuesday

Wednesday

Thursday

Friday

Saturday

Notes:

Notes:

Notes:

Notes:

Notes:

Notes:

Notes:

My Aspirations
THIS WEEK

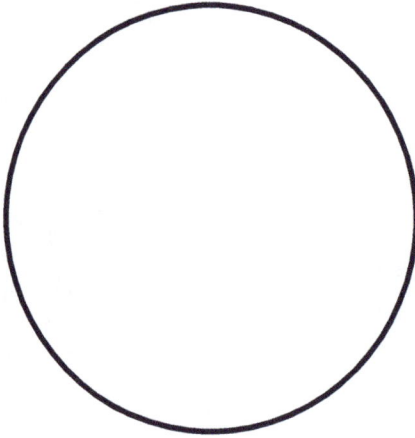

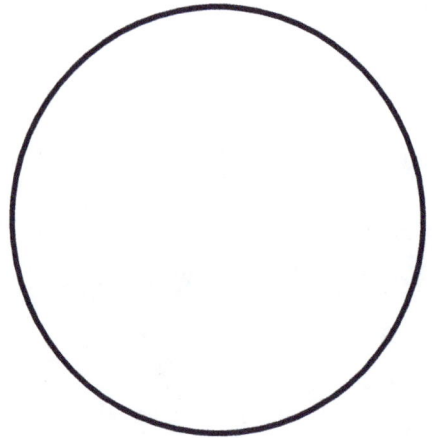

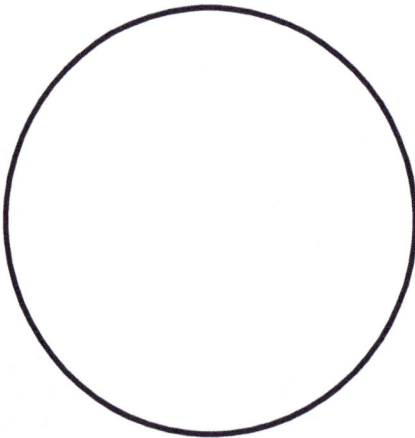

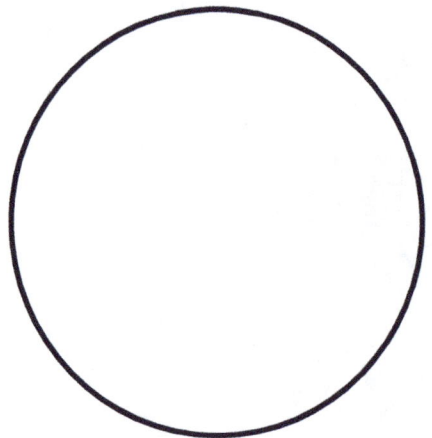

Journal

Journal

Journal

Free Art Space

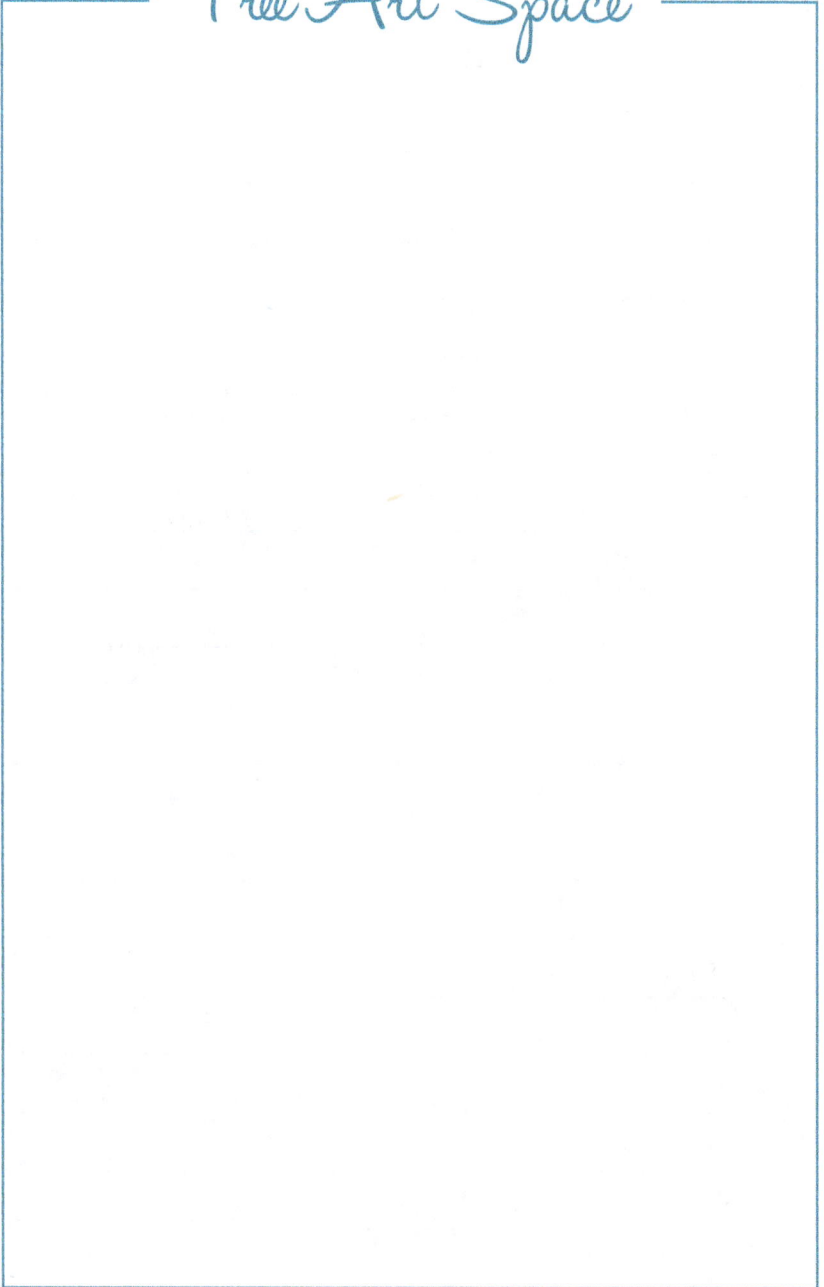

My Accomplishments
THIS MONTH

_____

_____

_____

_____

_____

_____

_____

Areas of Growth
FOR NEXT MONTH

_____

_____

_____

_____

_____

_____

_____

Sunday

Monday

Tuesday

Wednesday

Thursday

Friday

Saturday

Notes:

Notes:

Notes:

Notes:

Notes:

Notes:

Notes:

My Aspirations
THIS WEEK

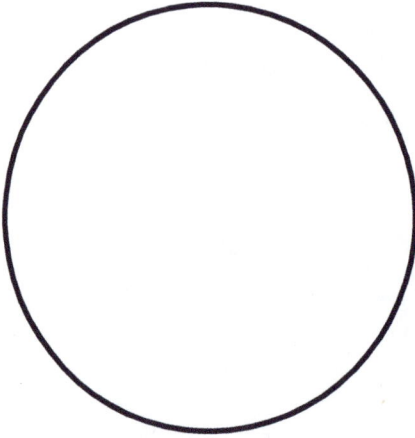

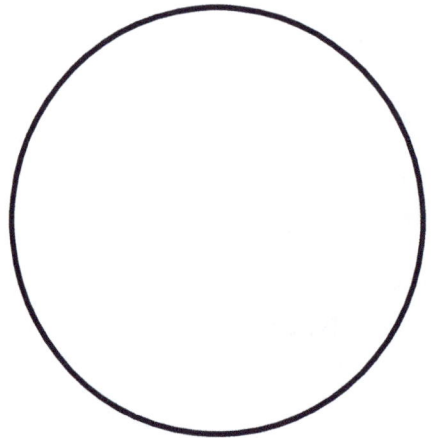

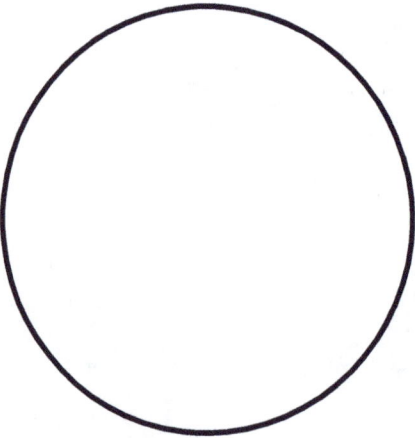

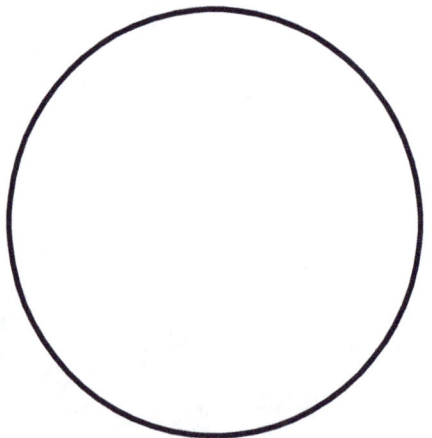

Journal

Journal

Week of:

Sunday

Monday

Tuesday

Wednesday

Thursday

Friday

Saturday

Notes:

Notes:

Notes:

Notes:

Notes:

Notes:

Notes:

My Aspirations
THIS WEEK

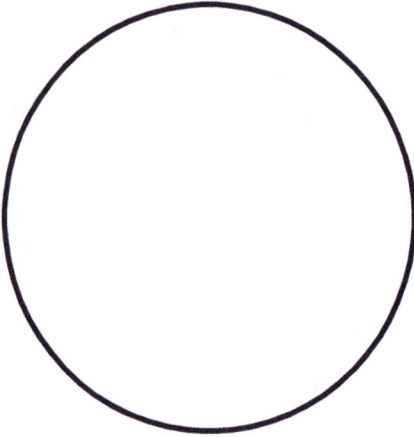

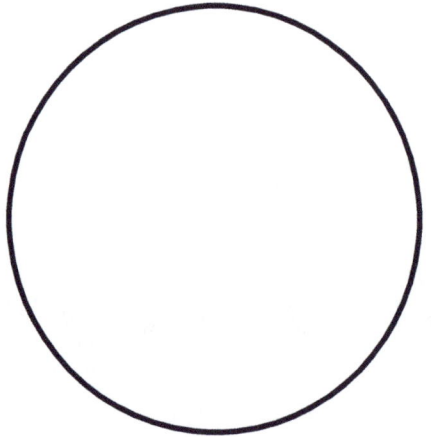

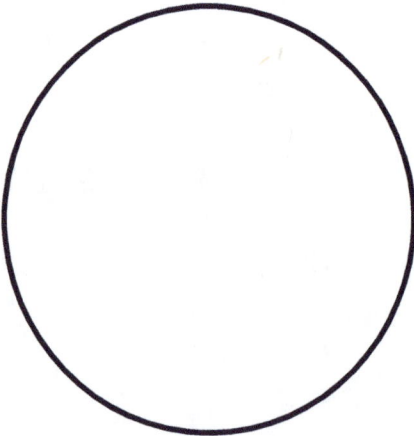

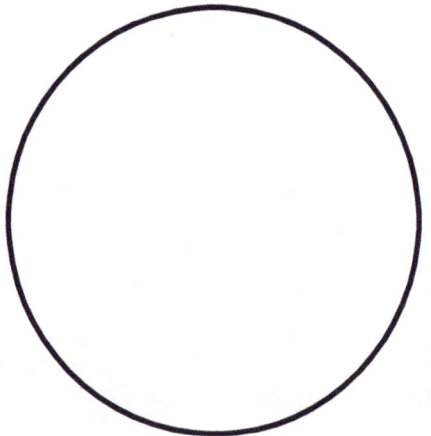

Journal

Journal

Free Art Space

Week of:

Sunday

Monday

Tuesday

Wednesday

Thursday

Friday

Saturday

Identify What is Meaningful to You

Notes:

Notes:

Notes:

Notes:

Notes:

Notes:

Notes:

My Aspirations
THIS WEEK

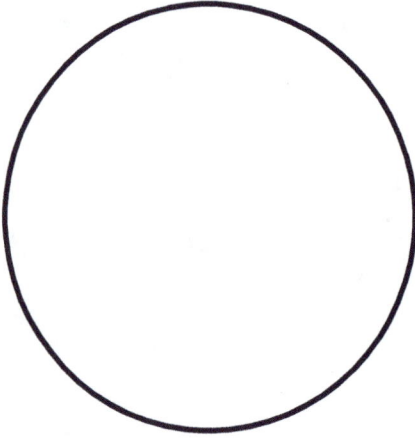

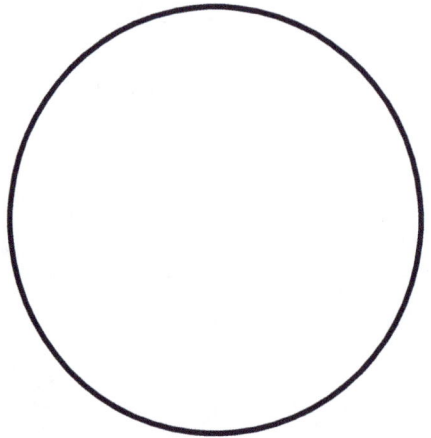

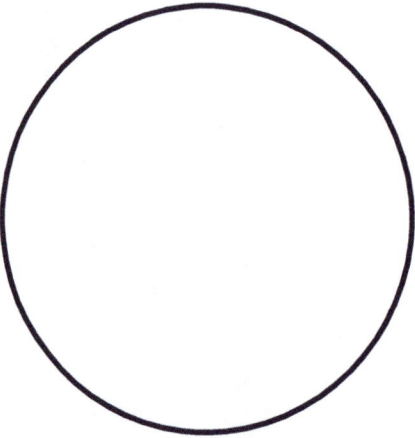

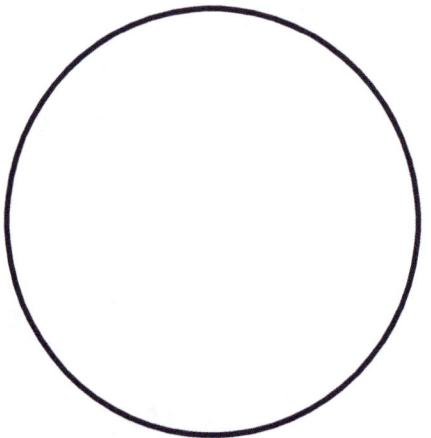

Journal

Journal

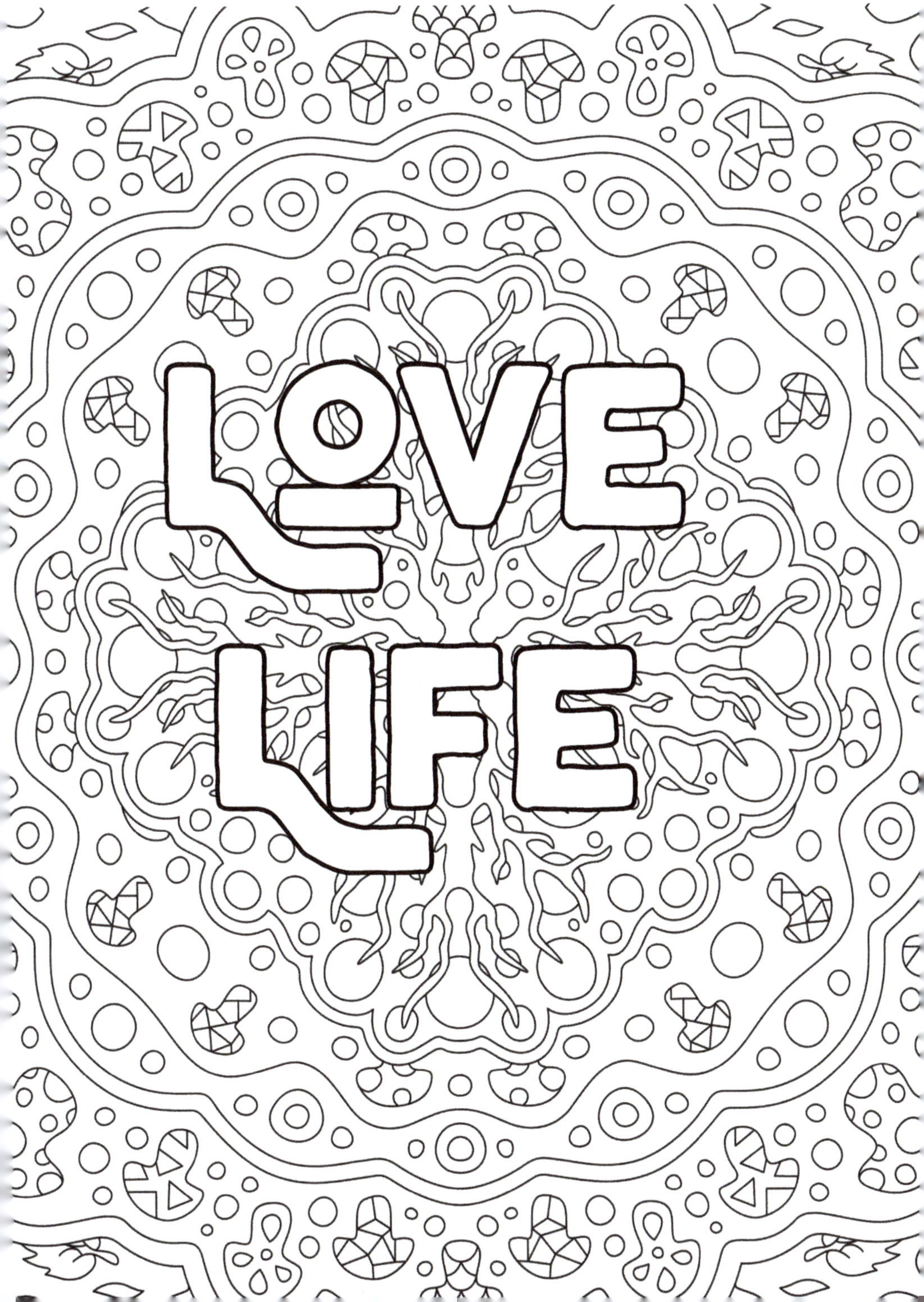
LOVE
LIFE

Week of:

Sunday

Monday

Tuesday

Wednesday

Thursday

Friday

Saturday

Wear Clothes That Are Becoming to You

Notes:

Notes:

Notes:

Notes:

Notes:

Notes:

Notes:

My Aspirations
THIS WEEK

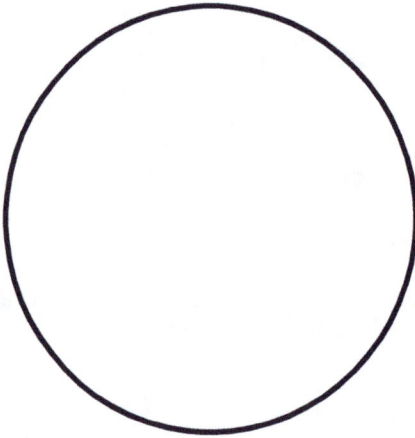

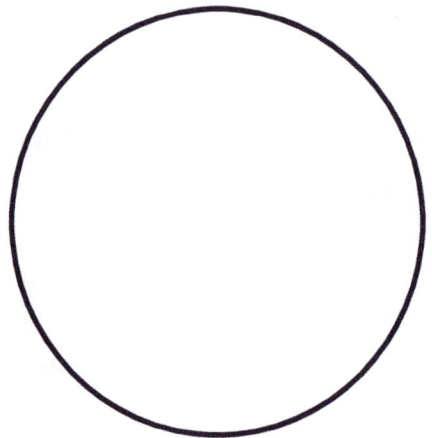

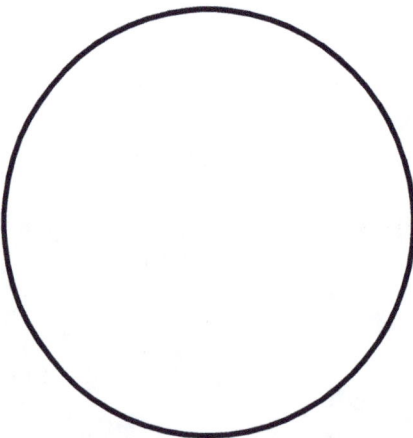

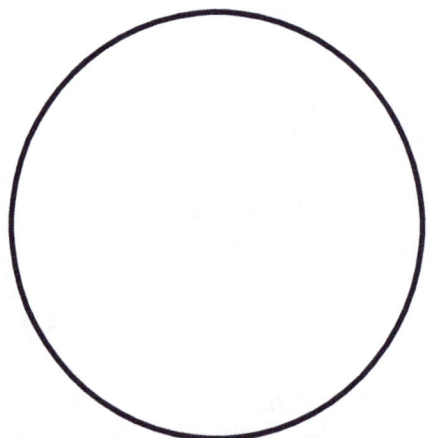

Journal

Journal

Journal

Free Art Space

My Accomplishments
THIS MONTH

_____
_____
_____
_____
_____
_____
_____
_____

Areas of Growth
FOR NEXT MONTH

_____
_____
_____
_____
_____
_____
_____
_____
_____

Week of:

Sunday

Monday

Tuesday

Wednesday

Thursday

Friday

Saturday

Notes:

Notes:

Notes:

Notes:

Notes:

Notes:

Notes:

My Aspirations
THIS WEEK

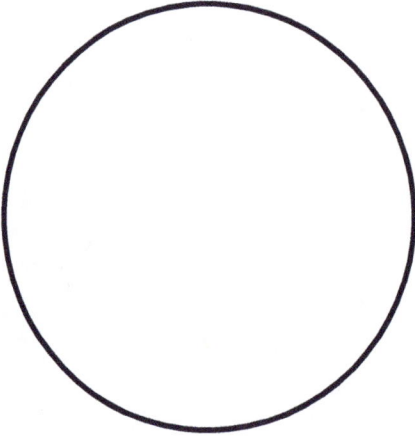

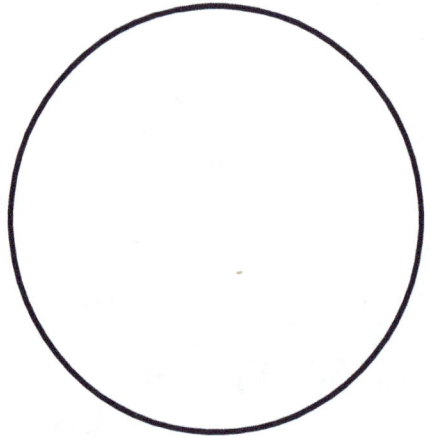

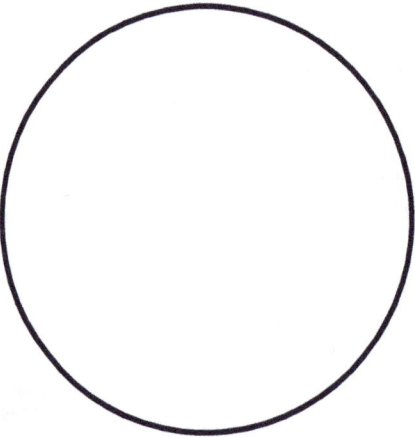

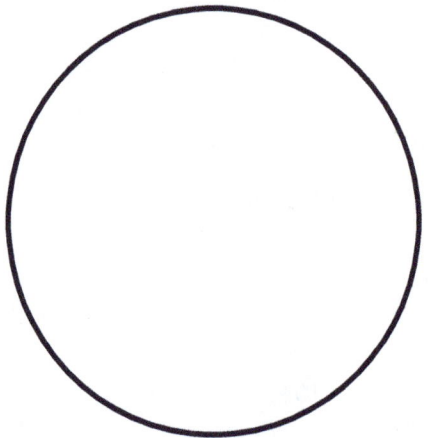

Journal

Journal

Sunday

Monday

Tuesday

Wednesday

Thursday

Friday

Saturday

Notes:

Notes:

Notes:

Notes:

Notes:

Notes:

Notes:

My Aspirations
THIS WEEK

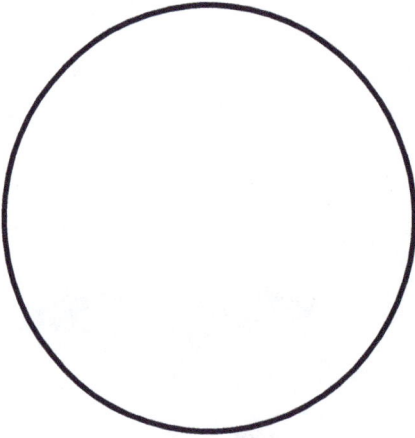

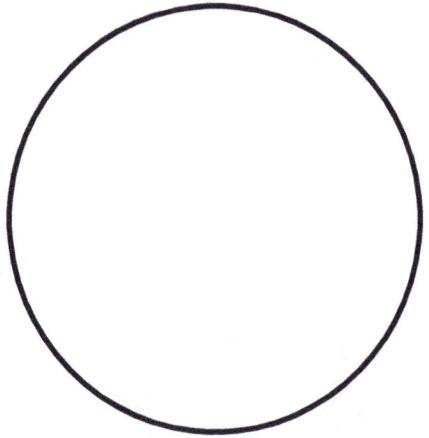

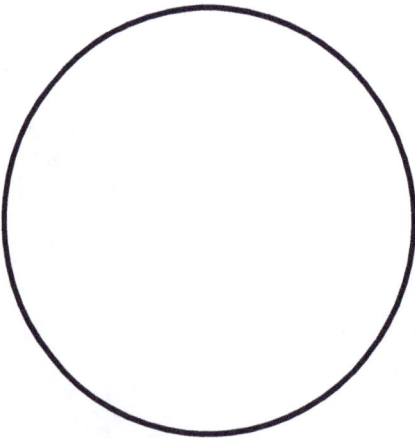

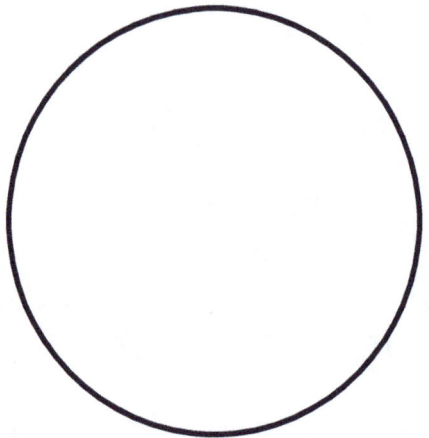

Journal

Journal

Free Art Space

Sunday

Monday

Tuesday

Wednesday

Thursday

Friday

Saturday

Notes:

Notes:

Notes:

Notes:

Notes:

Notes:

Notes:

My Aspirations
THIS WEEK

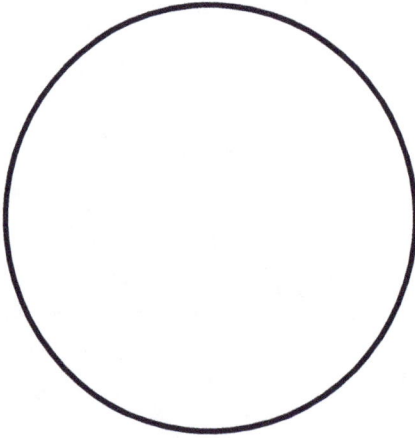

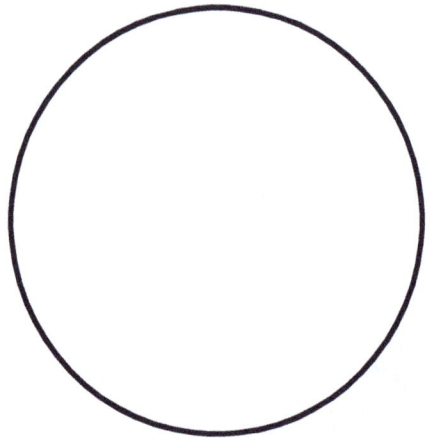

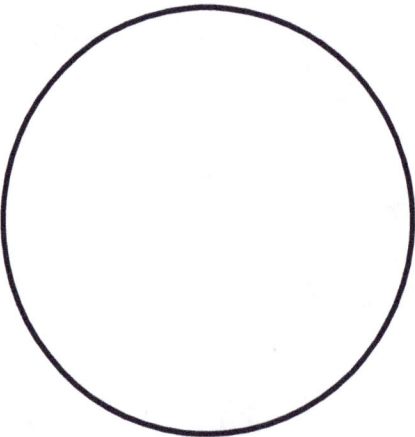

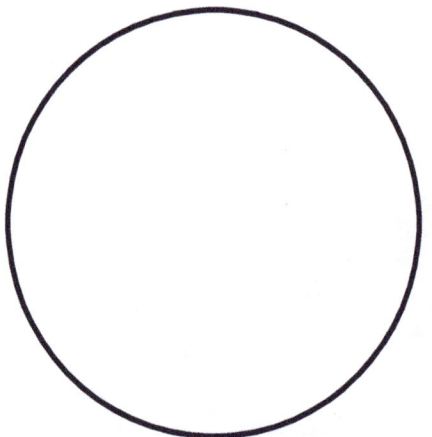

Journal

Journal

LOVE YOURSELF

Sunday

Monday

Tuesday

Wednesday

Thursday

Friday

Saturday

Amend Relationships Between People You Value

Notes:

Notes:

Notes:

Notes:

Notes:

Notes:

Notes:

My Aspirations
THIS WEEK

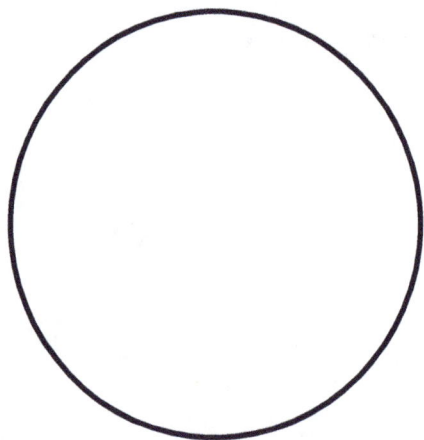

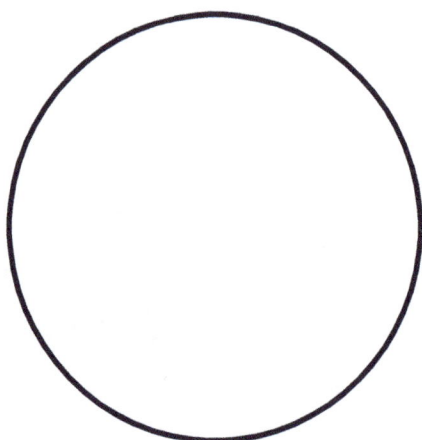

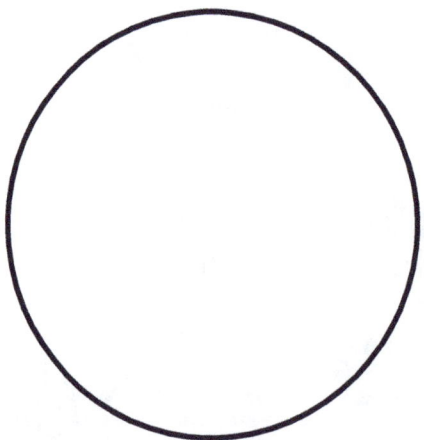

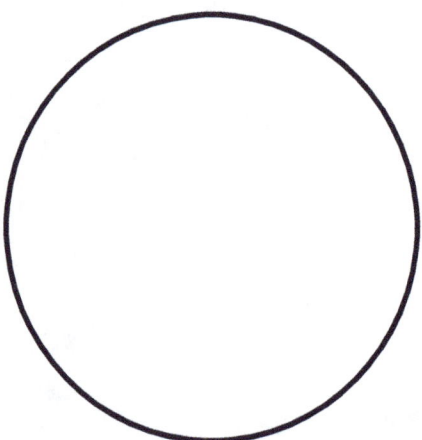

Journal

Journal

Journal

Free Art Space

My Accomplishments
THIS MONTH

_____

_____

_____

_____

_____

_____

_____

Areas of Growth
FOR NEXT MONTH

_____

_____

_____

_____

_____

_____

_____

Week of:

Sunday

Monday

Tuesday

Wednesday

Thursday

Friday

Saturday

Notes:

Notes:

Notes:

Notes:

Notes:

Notes:

Notes:

My Aspirations
THIS WEEK

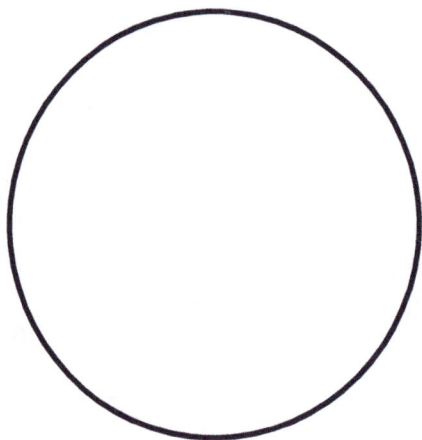

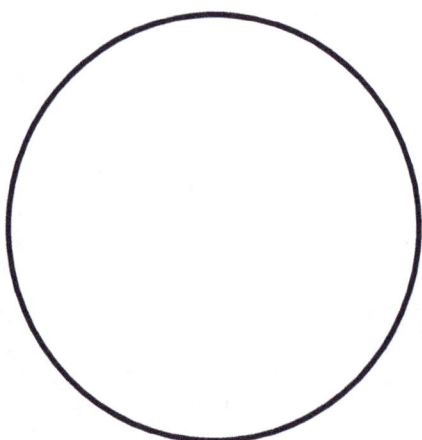

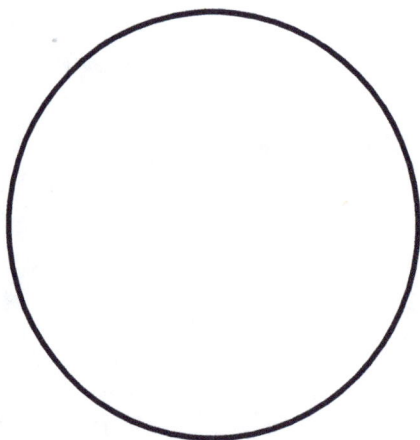

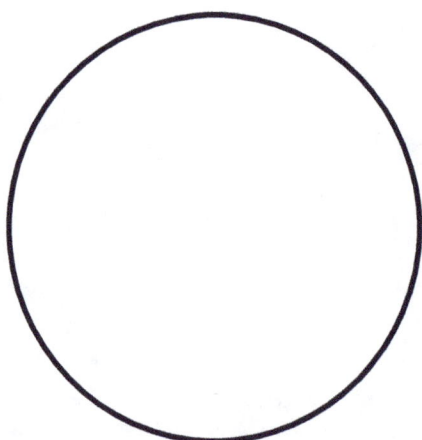

Journal

Journal

Week of:

Sunday

Monday

Tuesday

Wednesday

Thursday

Friday

Saturday

Notes:

Notes:

Notes:

Notes:

Notes:

Notes:

Notes:

My Aspirations
THIS WEEK

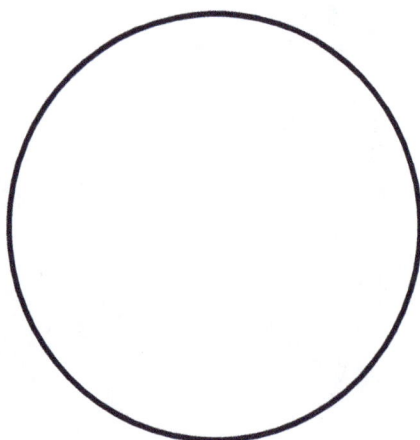

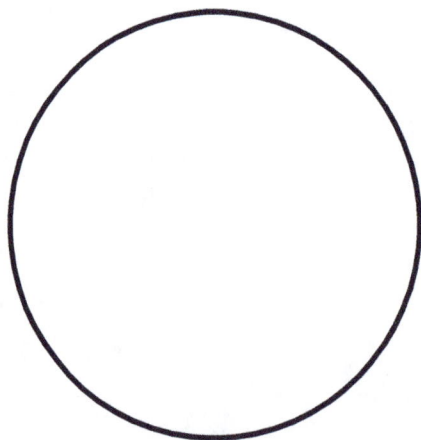

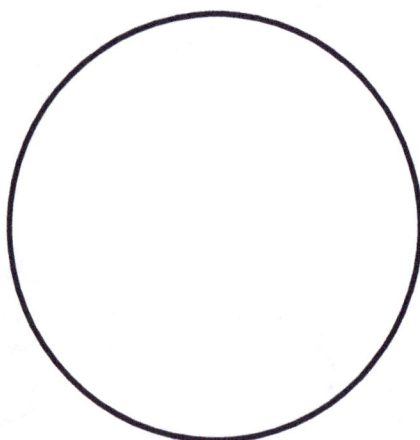

Journal

Journal

Free Art Space

Sunday

Monday

Tuesday

Wednesday

Thursday

Friday

Saturday

Notes:

Notes:

Notes:

Notes:

Notes:

Notes:

Notes:

My Aspirations
THIS WEEK

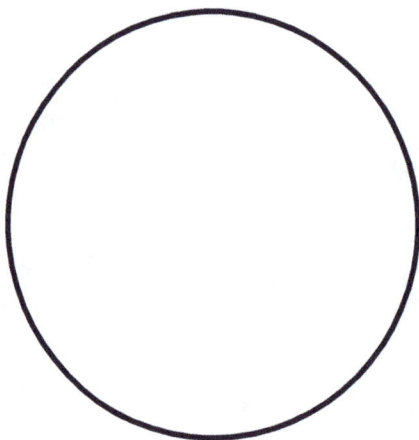

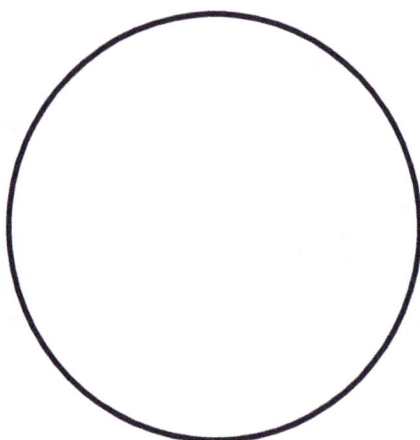

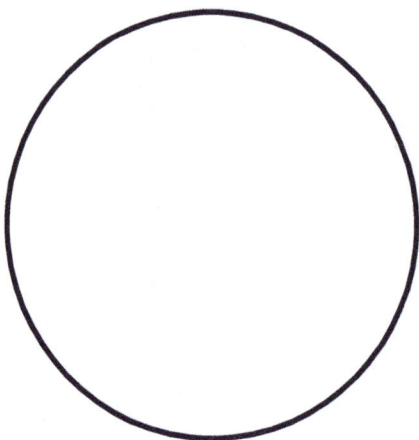

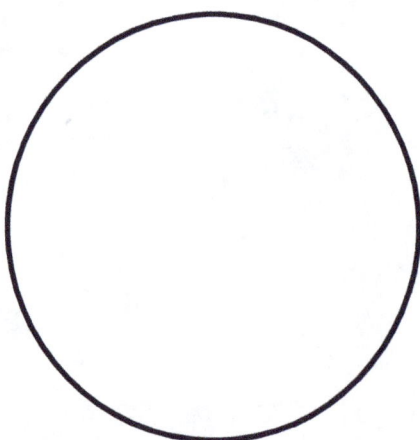

Journal

Journal

SELF
REFLECT

Week of:

Sunday

Monday

Tuesday

Wednesday

Thursday

Friday

Saturday

Notes:

Notes:

Notes:

Notes:

Notes:

Notes:

Notes:

My Aspirations
THIS WEEK

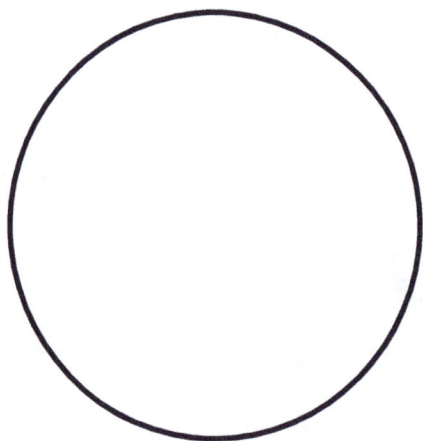

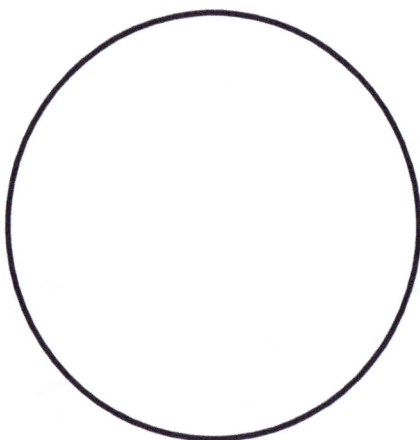

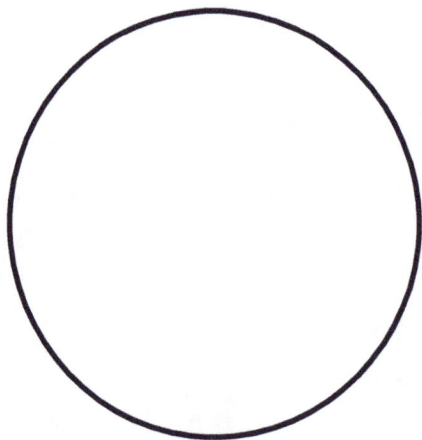

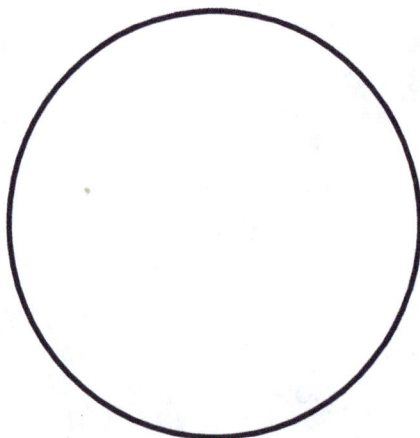

Journal

Journal

Journal

Free Art Space

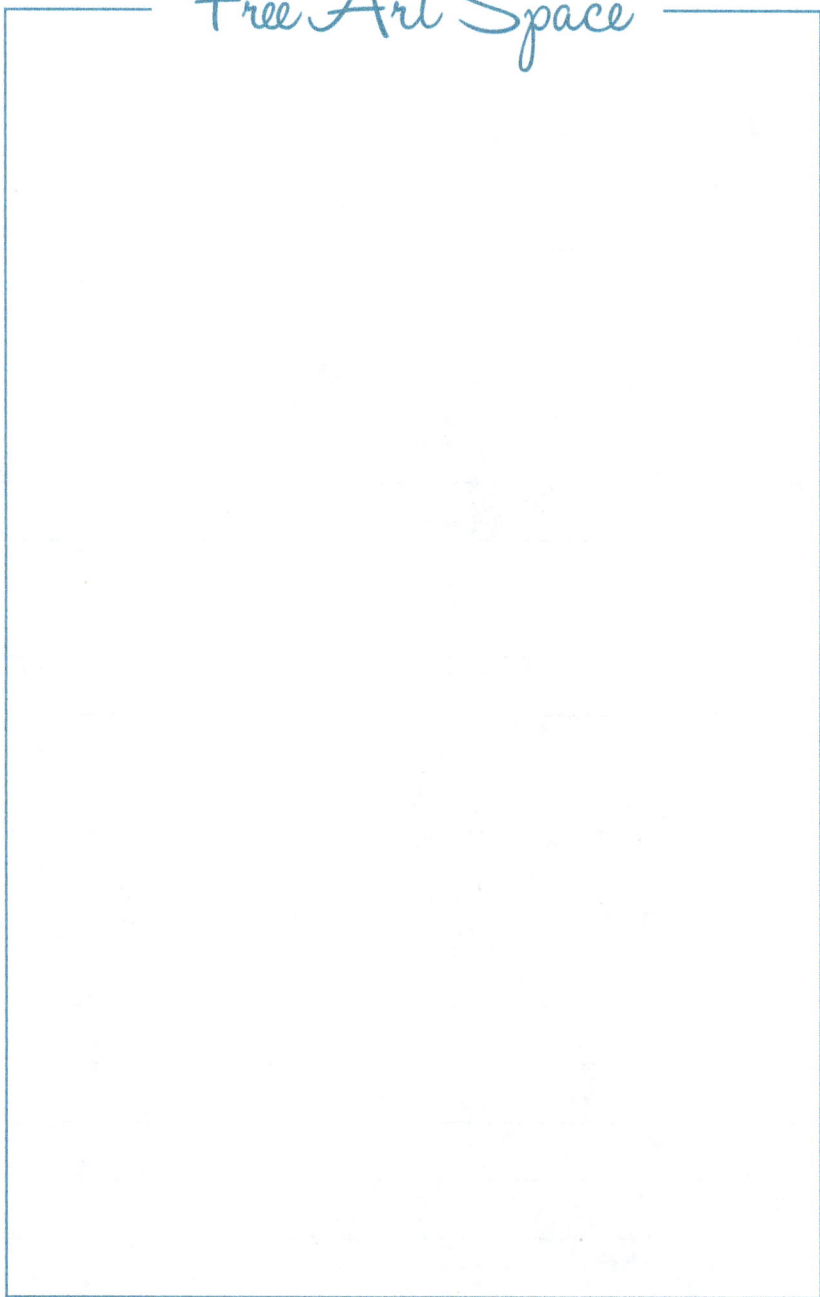

My Accomplishments
THIS MONTH

_____
_____
_____
_____
_____
_____
_____
_____
_____

Areas of Growth
FOR NEXT MONTH

_____
_____
_____
_____
_____
_____
_____
_____

Journal

Journal

Journal

Journal

Journal

Journal

Journal

Journal

Journal

Journal

Journal

Journal

Journal

Journal

Journal

Journal

Journal

Journal

Journal

Journal

Journal

Journal

Journal

Journal

Journal

Journal

About the Author

Kim Alderson, DSW, LCSW

Dr. Kimberly Alderson is a Licensed Clinical Social Worker and has worked in the field of Social Work for over 25 years. Through her podcast, individualized sessions, and group-based workshops, Dr. Alderson strives to inform and educate people about the power of self-care. These workshops provide education, awareness, empowerment, and elevation in the facet of self-care. This journal is Dr. Alderson's way of giving back what she has learned about self-care as she has studied this vast area.

Dr. Alderson thanks you and hopes that you will find this journal to be enlightening and helpful as you begin or continue your journey of self-care.

Learn More...

https://linktr.ee/afcpcdrkim

www.ingramcontent.com/pod-product-compliance
Lightning Source LLC
Chambersburg PA
CBHW060316100426
42812CB00003B/795